ROCKET
GENIUS

By Charles Spain Verral

Cover design by Robin Fight

Illustrated by Paul Frame

First published in 1963

This unabridged version has updated grammar and spelling.

© 2021 Jenny Phillips

goodandbeautiful.com

Table of Contents

1. False Alarm 1

2. The Beginning 6

3. Growing Up 10

4. The Balloon 15

5. The Move to Worcester. 20

6. The Cherry Tree 25

7. The Setback 31

8. The Experiment 36

9. The Report 41

10. Historymaker 46

11. Flight West. 52

12. The Space Age 56

Chapter 1

False Alarm

"Hello, police? This is an emergency! There's been an explosion. It shook all the window panes in my house . . ."

The woman's voice was shrill with excitement as it came over the telephone at police headquarters in Worcester, Massachusetts.

It was a few minutes past two o'clock on the afternoon of July 17, 1929. The police sergeant on duty had been dozing in the heat. But now he was wide awake.

"An explosion?" he asked sharply. "Where?"

"Out near Auburn," the woman said. "On the old Ward farm. There was an airplane … it was on fire in the sky. Then it crashed, and there was a terrible explosion. Send help! Hurry!"

The sergeant did just that. Within minutes, two

police cars and two ambulances were speeding away from the city of Worcester toward Auburn, three miles to the south. Following closely behind were more cars, filled with reporters from the Worcester newspapers.

The procession of cars raced over backcountry roads. When they reached the Ward farm, the cars turned into the lane. Ahead of them, trails of smoke could be seen rising in the sky. The cars sped past the farmhouse, the barnyard, and the barns. They kept on going along a narrow rutted road that dipped downhill through pastures to a ravine far below.

The police inspector was the first one out when the cars came to a stop in the ravine. He saw five men and a woman standing there, calmly talking. Near them, a large patch of grass had been burned away, and a film of smoke hung in the air. But there was no sign of a crashed airplane.

"Where's the plane?" the police inspector yelled.

The five men and the woman stared at him in surprise. Then one of them, a tall, balding man, stepped forward.

"Plane?" he said, frowning. "What plane?"

"We had a report that an airplane crashed in flames out here," the police officer said.

The tall man's puzzled look vanished. "Oh," he said. "Someone must have mistaken my rocket for an airplane. I guess it did make about as much noise as a plane."

"But this plane was on fire," the inspector said.

The tall man nodded. "Well, I suppose it might seem like that, with flames shooting out of the rocket's exhaust. I can see how someone might easily have thought my rocket was an airplane on fire."

By now the rest of the policemen and the reporters were crowding around.

"Your *rocket*?" one of the reporters said. He stared closely at the tall man's face. Then he snapped his fingers. "Of course! You're Professor Goddard of Clark University—the rocket man!"

"Yes," the tall man said. "I'm Dr. Goddard."

"You're the guy who once claimed you could shoot a rocket to the moon," the reporter went on excitedly. "So that's what happened! You shot off your moon rocket, and it exploded!"

"Nothing of the sort," Dr. Goddard replied. "This was simply a small experimental rocket. It went up about a hundred feet and then flew parallel to the ground for a short distance. When it came down, it smashed itself to bits, as I expected. This started a grass fire, which my assistants and I put out. That's all there was to it."

"Come on, Prof," the reporter said. "Don't try to kid us. We know it was your moon rocket."

Dr. Goddard shook his head. "I tell you there was no attempt to reach the moon or anything like that. True enough, I did say back in 1920 that it *might* be possible to send a rocket to the moon someday. But such a thing won't happen for many years to come."

Dr. Goddard might as well have been talking to himself. The reporters were not listening. They were heading back to their cars on the run.

The tall professor turned to his young blond wife. "Well, Esther," he said, gloomily, "I'm afraid we're in for another dose of wild stories like those I got back in 1920."

Dr. Goddard was right. When he and his wife drove back into Worcester two hours later, newsboys were on the street shouting, "Extra! Extra! Moon rocket blows up! Read all about it. Extra here!"

The exaggerated stories were printed not only in Worcester. The wire services picked up the news and spread it across the country. Headlines in the *St. Louis Post Dispatch* read: ROCKET STARTS FOR THE MOON BUT BLOWS UP ON WAY. There were even wilder accounts published abroad.

The commotion finally stirred up an official state investigation of Dr. Goddard's rocket tests. It was ruled that the Clark University professor would no longer be allowed to shoot off rockets anywhere in the state of Massachusetts because of the danger of starting brush or forest fires.

"Then we will go elsewhere," Dr. Goddard said firmly to his wife, Esther.

The idea of never sending up another rocket was

unthinkable to Dr. Goddard. He had been building and testing rockets for years. This had been his fourth successful launching. Others would follow, even if he had to go to the North Pole. He still had many questions he wanted answered about space. And he intended to find those answers with the help of his rockets.

Chapter 2

The Beginning

Robert Goddard had always been curious about everything. As a very small boy, he used to lie on his back in the grass behind his parents' house and stare up at the heavens.

He wondered about the clouds and the rain and where the winds came from and where they went. But mostly he wondered how high the sky was and what lay beyond it. He wanted to fly up there and find out for himself.

One day, when he was five years old, he tried.

At lunchtime his mother missed him. She went to the kitchen door.

"Bobbie!" she called. "Bobbie!"

There was no answer.

"Now where *is* that boy?" she muttered to herself.

It was not an easy question to answer. Her son

might be almost anywhere. He might be out in the yard watching an army of ants building an anthill. Or he could be in the shed inspecting the wonders of his father's tool chest.

Young Bob had recently become very interested in an electric battery his father owned. The sparks that shot out from it amazed him. His eyes grew large when his father spoke to him about the wonders of electricity. His father explained that anyone could make sparks, even without a battery. All one had to do was scuff his shoes hard on a carpet.

When Mrs. Goddard could not find her son in the backyard, she went to the front of the house. To her surprise, she saw Bob right away. But he was acting in a very odd manner. He scraped the soles of his shoes against the gravel of the front walk. Then he climbed up on a low picket fence and jumped off. He did this a number of times while his mother watched.

"Bobbie," Mrs. Goddard said as she walked out on the front porch, "what on earth are you doing?"

The little boy climbed up on the fence once more and jumped. Then he ran to his mother. Breathlessly, he told her that he was trying an experiment.

"What kind of an experiment?" Mrs. Goddard asked.

Bob patiently explained. He had taken a zinc rod from one of his father's old electric batteries. He had rubbed the rod many times back and forth against the soles of his shoes. Then he had scuffed his shoes against the gravel walk. He had reasoned that if the electric sparks that came from the battery could somehow be added to the sparks produced from the act of scuffing shoe leather, a great charge of electricity might be built up.

"It might be strong enough to send me up in the air, Mother," Bob said. "Maybe even up to the moon!"

His mother smiled. "Well, then," she said, "in that case you had better come in and eat your lunch. You'll need it. It's a long journey to the moon."

Five-year-old Bob thought that over and decided that perhaps he could do with a bite of lunch. After all, it would be a very long trip from Massachusetts to the moon.

Chapter 3

Growing Up

Massachusetts was Robert Hutchings Goddard's home state, as it had been his father's, his grandfather's, and his great-grandfather's before him. He was born there, in the city of Worcester, on October 5, 1882.

The year 1882 was an exciting year to come into the world. Chester Arthur was the new president in the White House. The French were trying to dig a canal across Panama. The Brooklyn Bridge was being built. And there were plans afoot to put up the giant Statue of Liberty in New York Harbor.

When Bob Goddard was less than a year old, his family moved from Worcester to Boston. This was because Bob's father, Nahum Goddard, had opened a small machine-tool factory there.

Bob had no brothers or sisters. As he grew up, he

often had to play by himself, especially when it was storming outside. But Bob had a lively imagination and had no trouble thinking of things to do. He learned to read at an early age. He liked stories of adventure, but mainly he liked books and magazines that had to do with science and with inventions.

Bob had a lot of curiosity. He wanted to know how everything worked. He would spend hours examining the wheels and springs inside a clock or inspecting the mechanism of his mother's sewing machine.

He asked his father so many questions that Nahum Goddard finally bought him a set of books called *Cassell's Popular Educator*. Later he got Bob a more advanced set, *Cassell's Technical Educator*.

"You stump me too often with your questions, son," his father said, smiling. "Maybe you'll find the answers in these books."

Bob usually hunted through the volumes until he did.

When Bob was in the fourth grade, he became interested in spiders and frogs. This happened after a summer when he and his father had taken many long tramps through the woods. Although Bob was filled with wonder at the way spiders spin their webs, it was the frogs that really captured his fancy. In fact, he decided that he would devote his life to raising frogs.

He drew up plans for a little house where his frogs would be hatched. He designed a system of water wheels and pumps so that water would flow through the house. He made working drawings of the hatchery, and when he was fourteen, he actually built a house for his frogs. It was painted gray with red trim and had small windows of real glass.

However, Bob's idea of making a career of raising frogs was never carried out. By the time he had completed his frog hatchery, his interest had swung to something new.

Bob had so many interests as he grew older that sometimes they almost crowded on top of one another. Usually he worked at one thing at a time until he was good at it—then he went on to something else.

He practiced shooting with an air rifle until he could hit a half-inch target at fifteen feet. He turned the attic of the Goddard house into a chemistry laboratory, and once, while trying to make artificial diamonds, he almost blew the roof off.

Bob also liked to draw and paint and to write stories and poems. He learned to play the cornet, the violin, and the piano. In his spare time, he sang in the choir of St. Anne's Episcopal Church.

In spite of all of his other interests, Bob never forgot the one that gripped him most. He kept trying to learn all he could about flight and about space.

Bob built himself a strong bow of seasoned oak and made special arrows for it. He was able to shoot the arrows to heights of one and two hundred feet. He wished he could send them much higher.

"There's one way to do it," Bob said to his friend Chester Haynes one day. "If only I could find a way to give each arrow an *extra push* every time it begins to lose forward speed—then it would keep going."

"Sure," Chester agreed. "That would keep 'em going up all right."

"Not only that," Bob went on, his eyes brightening. "The higher the arrow goes, the thinner the air will be. And the thinner the air, the faster the arrow will go because the air won't hold it back. See?"

"Sure I see," Chester said. "But ..."

Bob grabbed his friend excitedly by the arm. "Chester," he said, "it really should be possible to shoot an arrow into space ... maybe even as far as the moon and Mars!"

"Wait a minute," Chester said. "I've been trying to tell you that there's just one hitch. How are you going to give the arrow those extra shoves when you're down here and it's up there?"

The light faded from Bob's eyes. "Yes, I guess it is a pretty wild idea," he admitted. "But, I'll think of a way to do it someday. You'll see!"

Chapter 4

The Balloon

Bob also built kites to explore the sky. He flew them in all kinds of weather and for hours at a time. When it was a fine day, he usually had a group of little children tagging along. Often he would let one of them hold the string of his high-flying kite.

The airplane had not been invented when Bob was growing up. The only way a person could fly was by balloon. Bob read everything he could find about ballooning. And when balloonists put on exhibitions at county fairs around Boston, Bob was usually on hand to watch the big gas bags go up.

One snowy night in December 1897, as he lay warm and snug in his bed, fifteen-year-old Bob reached a decision. He would build a balloon himself. It would not be a toy balloon of rubber or silk. It would be made of aluminum and filled with hydrogen. Once launched, *his* balloon would stay up in the sky for a long time.

Bob began to save every penny he could spare from his weekly allowance of forty cents. He kept a diary in those days, and on January 8, 1898, he wrote, "Went and got ½ lb. of aluminum. Tried to melt it nearly all day but could not."

His idea was to turn the molten aluminum into a thin sheet. He planned to roll this sheet into a large, hollow ball. On January 10, he wrote in his diary: "After school tried to melt aluminum again but could not."

The family plumber finally advised Bob to give up trying to melt the aluminum and to buy it in sheet form. Bob took the advice. He sold back the half-pound of aluminum to the man from whom he had bought it. He did not lose a penny on the deal, either.

On January 18, he wrote: "After school went and bought 3 ft. of sheet aluminum for 54 cents."

The sheet was one-hundredth of an inch thick— about the thickness of a fingernail. Bob was sure his troubles were over now. But he soon found out that it was far from easy to mold the sheet of aluminum into the shape he wanted. Each day he hurried home from school to work on his balloon. He finally gave up trying to make it into a round shape. Instead, he settled for a balloon that was pillow shaped.

Now Bob faced a new problem: How could he seal the edges of his balloon together? Bob went to his reference books to find suggestions on how to cement aluminum. Finally, he bought some yellow powder called litharge and mixed it with glycerine, a solvent. On January 27, he noted triumphantly: "After school cemented aluminum."

Bob had a close friend named Jim Young. Jim had shown interest in the balloon. And whenever he could, Jim came over to the Goddards' to help Bob work on it. Jim did not have too much spare time, however. He had a job after school and on Saturdays in a neighborhood drugstore.

Now that Bob had sealed his balloon, hope of success began to run high. The two boys agreed to launch the balloon on the following Saturday. The launching would take place outside the drugstore. Jim could stay on his job and still slip out to help if Bob needed him.

It was raining on Saturday morning, but Bob was determined to go ahead with the plan in spite of the weather. The balloon was an armful, yet Bob managed to carry it from his home to the drugstore. He put it down on the sidewalk. Jim was waiting for him in the doorway.

The boys had bought a small tank of hydrogen gas and had arranged for it to be delivered to the launching site. Bob crouched down and fitted a tube from the hydrogen cylinder into an opening at the side of the balloon. Jim held his hand on the cylinder's valve. He kept glancing nervously into the drugstore.

His boss, the druggist, was a patient man, but there
was a limit to his patience.

"All right," Bob said. "Turn her on."

Jim flipped over the valve handle, and the hydrogen
began to hiss into the balloon. Bob's heart was

hammering so hard he was sure it would knock a hole through his ribs. The great moment was at hand.

The boys had wound a heavy cord around the balloon and then tied it to a lamppost. This was to keep the balloon from soaring away when it began to rise.

But the balloon did not move upward—not even a fraction of an inch.

A crowd had gathered. "What did you make that thing out of, kid?" somebody asked. "Pig iron?"

That brought a big laugh.

Bob flushed. It was all too clear what had happened. The aluminum was just too heavy for the hydrogen to lift. The balloon might as well have been nailed to the ground.

That night Bob wrote in his diary: "Aluminum balloon will not go up. Failior crowns enterprise."

His misspelling of the word "failure" did not bother Bob. But the dashing of his hopes did. He had dreamed of launching a glittering silver balloon high over Boston.

His disappointment, however, was soon forgotten, and within a day Bob was going full steam ahead on a new project.

Chapter 5

The Move to Worcester

Bob lived in Boston for the first sixteen years of his life. He had a good time there. He and his parents were happy together in their comfortable, big house. His father's factory was doing well. Bob liked his school and his schoolmates.

In many ways, Bob was a very lucky boy. Almost everything he did was approved of by his parents, especially by his father. Nahum Goddard had an inventive mind himself, and he was delighted with Bob's scientific experiments and other projects. He did all he could to encourage his son.

When Bob showed an interest in astronomy, his father bought him a telescope. When Bob began to write stories and poems, he was given a typewriter. This was at a time when typewriters were far from common and were rarely seen outside of a business office.

Bob's budding talent as an artist was aided by sets of oil paints and watercolors. His father provided Bob with the proper tools for carpentry work and the right equipment for chemistry. When Bob developed a taste for music, he was given not only a cornet, a violin, and a piano, but Nahum Goddard bought him a phonograph as well.

A phonograph in those days was a real luxury. After all, only a few years had passed since Thomas A. Edison had invented his wonderful "talking machine."

Bob could easily have been spoiled by all the attention he received. But he was not. Instead, he made use of every advantage that his father gave him. Bob and his father understood each other. They had a firm friendship.

Nahum Goddard was a slim, bald man with a quick smile and a good sense of humor. When he came home from the factory in the late afternoon, he could be heard a block away whistling a gay tune. At suppertime he usually had a funny story to tell.

But for all the gaiety and laughter in the house at 63 Forest Street, Boston, there was sadness and worry too. Bob's mother was a very sick woman. She had tuberculosis.

Tuberculosis (or TB, as it is called) was a dreadful disease in those days. A great many people suffered from it. Some were sent to special hospitals, called sanatoriums, where they often spent months in bed. Others tried to recover at home.

Bob's mother stayed home. She had periods when she would be up and around and, apparently, on her way back to good health. Then the fever would return and so would the cough.

To make matters worse, Bob was sick a lot too. He had stomach trouble and many colds. He was absent from school a great deal.

Time after time he wrote in his diary: "Stayed in on account of cold in my head." "Had biliousness all day and stayed in bed. Doctor came." "Stayed in bed all day—liver."

In the spring of 1899, Mrs. Goddard's illness took a serious turn. Doctors came and went. Nurses were on duty around the clock. It was soon quite clear that Bob's mother would not be able to keep up the big house in Boston, even with the help of a servant. The doctors advised complete rest and good, clean country air.

The family decided to move back to Worcester, forty miles away. There they would live with Bob's grandmother in her roomy old farmhouse at the edge of town. It was the house where Bob had been born and where he had spent most of his summers.

Bob loved the farmhouse, and he loved "Gram." But it was still a wrench to leave Boston and to say goodbye to his loyal friends, Chester and Jim. Bob had just completed his first year at the English High School in Boston, and he did not look forward to going to a new school where he would not know anyone. But, as

it turned out, Bob did not go to a new school in
Worcester the following fall. He did not go to school at
all.

The move to Grandmother Goddard's soon proved
to be of great benefit to Bob's mother. Within weeks

she began to look and feel better. But Bob was not so fortunate. His stomach trouble returned and with it came a severe kidney ailment.

Once again he was put to bed, and the family doctor was called. The doctor examined Bob. Then he called in specialists to examine Bob, too. Sick as he was, Bob grew very restless as doctor after doctor asked him questions and prodded and poked him.

"Well, there's just one thing to do," the family doctor finally told Bob's father. "He's a mighty sick boy. He'll have to take it easy for some time and get plenty of rest."

"But school!" Nahum Goddard said. "What about school?"

"No school for Bob this year, I'm afraid," the doctor said.

So Bob stayed home and rested and rested until he was tired of resting. By late fall he was better and was allowed to go out of the house for short periods. After a while, Bob was able to rake up fallen leaves and do other outdoor work.

That was when the dream came to him—the amazing dream that was to guide and shape his whole life.

Chapter 6

The Cherry Tree

Bob's dream was not the kind you have at night when your eyes are closed and you are asleep. He was wide awake when he had this one. It was a daydream.

The daydream came to him on Thursday afternoon, October 19, 1899, when he was seventeen. It was a fine, clear day with a nip of autumn in the air. Bob was out for a stroll around his grandmother's farm. As he walked past the orchard, he noticed that a tall cherry tree needed pruning.

Bob got a saw and a hatchet. He climbed the tree and began to cut off the small dead branches. He was still quite weak from his illness, and he had to rest every so often.

From his perch high in the tree, the ground below looked very far away. Bob began to imagine that he was in some sort of flying machine. It seemed to him that the machine was being sent up into the sky by a

secret device that allowed it to escape the pull of the earth's gravity.

This daydream was so real to Bob that he could almost see the machine soaring into outer space.

He later wrote: "It was one of those quiet, colorful

afternoons of sheer beauty which we have in October in New England, and as I looked toward the field of the east, I imagined how wonderful it would be to make some device which had even the possibility of ascending to Mars, and how it would look on a small scale if sent up from the meadow at my feet."

He was never quite sure how long his dream lasted. But when he did climb down to the ground, he was, as he wrote, "a different boy when I descended the tree from when I ascended." He was now certain what his life's work would be: the exploration of space.

As long as he lived, Bob never forgot that afternoon in 1899. October 19 became Anniversary Day to him. He never let the date pass unnoticed. If he was in Worcester, he would walk to the cherry tree. Sometimes he would climb up into it. Sometimes he would just stand there and think. If he was far away, he would spend a few quiet moments remembering.

Bob's health improved during the year he was out of school, but not enough to satisfy the family doctor. Much to Bob's disgust, he had to remain at home for another school year.

Even though Bob's body was forced to be inactive, his brain certainly was not. His bedroom began to look like a cross between a science laboratory and a machine shop. He carved propellers from wood, experimented with parachutes, and built a model of a turbine windmill. He watched the flight of swallows through his telescope and carefully sketched the movement of their wings.

Bob spent many hours observing Venus, Mars, and the moon through his telescope. He read books on the atmosphere, on the theory of flight, on astronomy, and on anything that had to do with high altitude.

Bob had not done too well in mathematics during his first year of high school in Boston. Now he realized that if he were to become a "space scientist," he would have to be good in both mathematics and physics. He began to study on his own.

Bob was at last allowed to go to Worcester South High School in the fall of 1901. He wrote in his journal: "I resolved to lead the class in geometry and managed to do so."

Worcester South High School had just been built the year that Bob entered. He was delighted with the modern equipment and enthusiastic teachers. Even so, returning to school after an absence of two years was difficult for Bob. He was nineteen, at least two years older than most of his classmates. Also, he was now almost six feet tall, and he towered over the other students in his class.

Yet it did not take Bob long to get into the swing of things. He liked people and they liked him. He quickly became one of the school crowd. In his first term at school, he was elected vice president of his class. He sang in the South High quartet and played the piano for class dances.

Bob's three years at South High were happy ones. The old gaiety had returned to the Goddard household, and their serious troubles seemed a thing of the past.

When Bob was a senior, he was a man of twenty-one. Most of his classmates were still boys. It was no wonder that they elected him class president. His many years of so much reading in bed also paid off, and his teachers chose Bob to give the oration at graduation.

Bob was nervous as he stood up on the platform of Mechanics Hall in Worcester on the afternoon of June 24, 1904. The place was filled with parents and friends of the graduating class.

Nahum Goddard was there in one of the front seats, smiling proudly. Gram was there too. But Bob's mother was not. She had been too weak to come, but she had heard Bob's speech in advance. He had rehearsed it in her bedroom the night before.

"It's wonderful, Bobbie," she had said gently, patting his hand. "Just wonderful."

It was a good speech, and once Bob got going, he forgot his nervousness. He spoke of the great advances that had been made in the world of science. He spoke, too, of the even greater inventions and discoveries that were to come.

Bob ended his speech with the thought: "The dream of yesterday is the hope of today and the reality of tomorrow."

   As to Bob's own private dream, it was growing
brighter than ever, and he was eager to follow
wherever it led.

Chapter 7

The Setback

The dream led Bob straight to Worcester Polytechnic Institute the following September. He entered the institute on a scholarship and remained there for four years.

"Tech" was Bob's kind of place. Even though the carefree fun of high school was over, Bob did not mind. He was hungry to learn, and he threw himself into his studies.

Whenever he had a free moment from classes, he turned to his own special interest: space. He bought a number of green cloth-covered notebooks. In them he jotted down every idea that came into his mind concerning the upper reaches of the sky.

Bob's thoughts and theories about space crept into his work at Tech. Time and again he was crushed when his instructors flatly turned down his ideas. On

March 4, 1906, in his second year at Tech, he wrote
in the deepest gloom: "Decided today that space
navigation is a physical impossibility."

Yet the ink had scarcely dried in his diary when he
was busy working on a new and different theory about
how man might someday travel safely in space.

During his years at Tech, Bob became interested
in fireworks, mainly skyrockets. He was impressed by
the way a rocket could streak high into the heavens,
spouting a trail of fire, and how it kept on going until
its fuel of black powder was burned up.

"Rockets!" he muttered half to himself while he
watched a fireworks display one Independence Day.
"Maybe that's the answer!"

"What are you mumbling about?" a Tech student
beside him asked. "What's the answer?"

Bob did not reply. He was thinking back to the
time when he and his friend Chester had talked about
shooting an arrow into outer space—if only it could
be given an extra push when it slowed down. Bob
had long since given up the arrow idea. But now he
began wondering if he could give a rocket those "extra
pushes." Would it keep on going?

Perhaps, Bob reasoned, two or more rockets
fastened together would do the trick and would go
much higher than one rocket alone. The rockets could
be fastened one behind the other, like railroad cars.
Then, if the rocket at the rear was fired first, it would

carry the other rockets in front of it along as it shot skyward. When the rear rocket's fuel was used up and reached the top of its climb, it would detach itself and drop back to Earth while the next rocket in line would be fired and would keep on going up. If there was a third rocket, it would work in the same manner.

Bob hurried away to his room. He made a quick drawing of the combination rocket he had imagined. Years later this type of rocket was to become known as the step, or multistage, rocket.

On September 15, 1907, Bob had an experience that he never forgot.

"Today," he wrote in his diary, "I rode in an auto."

Even though Bob was beginning to develop the basic ideas of manned rocket flight which would send people speeding through space at over eighteen thousand miles an hour, he was thrilled to be riding in a "gasoline buggy" at about fifteen miles an hour.

Bob graduated with a bachelor of science degree from Worcester Polytechnic Institute on June 11, 1908. He wrote: "Graduated from Tech in a.m. Got first prize, $75, and a handshake."

Bob had hoped to enter Clark University in Worcester the following fall to do graduate work. But the illness of his mother had been so costly that he wanted to spare his father any extra expense. So Bob got busy and had himself appointed an instructor in physics at Tech.

After a year of lecturing and teaching, Bob had saved enough money to enter Clark in the autumn of 1909. He had a world of ideas to talk over with his professors, and many more that were so advanced he had to keep them to himself.

In 1910 Bob received his master's degree from Clark University, and one year later his doctor of philosophy degree. He was now Doctor Robert Goddard.

There was a special dinner at home that night. Bob's mother was allowed to get out of bed to attend.

"Hip hip hooray!" Nahum Goddard said as Bob entered the dining room. Mr. Goddard grinned at his wife and at Gram. "Just think, we have a doctor of our own in the house."

"Dr. Bob" wanted to keep on with his experiments at Clark, so he arranged to stay there and use the laboratory for the next year. He began to work more and more with rockets. He clamped them to stands and then fired them off. In this way, he was able to measure how much thrust or power they had without the rockets actually taking off through the lab ceiling.

Even firing captive rockets was a risky business. Sometimes there were violent explosions. More than once, a fire alarm was turned in by some passerby who saw black smoke billowing from the windows of the physics laboratory.

A great honor came to Dr. Bob in 1912. He was offered a research fellowship at Princeton University, and he jumped at the chance.

If he had worked hard before, he worked doubly hard now in his eagerness to find the secrets of space. He spent all day in the laboratory and often worked late into the night, too.

The long hours of work had their effect on Dr. Bob. When he went back to Worcester to spend Easter vacation in 1913, he had a bad cold and felt worn out and miserable.

Bob was running a temperature, and as soon as he arrived home, he was put to bed. The family doctor was called. After an examination, he decided to call in a specialist. There was another examination.

"You both look mighty serious," Dr. Bob said to the medical men. "What's the trouble?"

"I'm afraid that you're in serious trouble this time, Bob," the family doctor said. "You have tuberculosis of both lungs."

They did not tell him then, but he found out later that he had been given only two weeks to live.

Chapter 8

The Experiment

Dr. Bob was far from ready to die. He had too much work to do.

"They aren't going to write me off yet," he said when he finally heard the medical report. "I'm going to get well."

He knew that he was in for a long, hard battle. People did not get over tuberculosis quickly, if at all. However, his health soon began to improve. In two weeks his temperature was back to normal. Even so, he was under strict orders to do nothing but rest.

He had all of his books and papers sent home from Princeton and brought to his room. When he had been at Princeton, Dr. Bob had been too busy to make a careful review of all that he had accomplished during the year. But now, lying in bed, he was able to go over everything slowly and carefully. The result was that he decided to try to have some of his rocket ideas patented in Washington.

For a month or so, he was not allowed to do so much as lift a pen. Then, as he became stronger, he was permitted to work one hour a day, but no more.

"During May," Dr. Bob put down in his diary, "I wrote the material for the U.S. patents which cover the essentials of rocket propulsion."

He was granted these patents the following year. They had to do with a system of sending fuel into a rocket's combustion (or burning) chamber, an exhaust nozzle to funnel off the escaping gases, and his idea for a step, or multistage, rocket.

If anything good could be said about Dr. Bob's illness, it was that it gave him the chance to apply for these basic patents. Otherwise he might have lost the rights to his inventions.

Dr. Bob made slow but steady progress in his fight for health. By the fall of 1914, he had recovered enough to teach physics part-time at Clark University and to resume his rocket experiments.

There was one experiment in particular that Bob was anxious to try. He wanted to prove that a rocket could operate in the vacuum of outer space.

In those days, most people, even scientists, thought that such a thing as space flight was impossible. They believed that a rocket was propelled forward by the force of its exhaust gases pushing back against the earth's air or atmosphere. The theory that a rocket could fly through space, where there was no air for it to push against, was not taken seriously by the experts.

Dr. Bob was convinced that the experts were wrong. He believed that a rocket could keep going without

pushing back against anything. Dr. Bob based his thinking on a principle that had been stated centuries before by the great scientist Sir Isaac Newton in his Third Law of Motion.

Dr. Bob had read Newton's Third Law of Motion in *Cassell's Popular Educator,* the set of books his father had given him as a young boy. He knew the law by heart: *For every action, there is an equal and opposite reaction.*

He knew, too, that every time he had shot his air rifle as a boy, he had felt the Third Law in operation. When the gun was fired and the lead pellet sped out of the barrel, the butt end of the gun recoiled, or kicked back, against his shoulder. The gun's recoil proved Newton's Third Law. The action of the compressed air sending the pellet out of the barrel caused the equal and opposite reaction of the recoil.

Dr. Bob believed that a rocket operated in the very same way as a gun. He was sure that the action of the gases escaping from a rocket's burning fuel caused a reaction in the other direction. He reasoned that, as the gas shot out of the rocket's exhaust nozzle at the rear, the "thrust," or kick, would make the rocket spurt forward. Dr. Bob was certain that a rocket's forward motion had nothing to do with pushing back against the air, or anything else.

To prove to himself that he was right, Dr. Bob set up an experiment. He fired a pistol into the air and measured its recoil. Then he put the pistol into a vacuum—a sealed chamber from which all the air had been pumped out. He fired the pistol by using a switch outside the chamber.

To his great satisfaction, the pistol kicked backward. If anything, the recoil was greater in the vacuum than in ordinary air. Dr. Bob had all the proof he needed. Now he knew that a rocket could work as well, if not better, in outer space than in the earth's atmosphere.

Knowing this, his immediate problem was to work toward building a type of rocket that would be powerful enough to climb up through the atmosphere and reach outer space.

"I'm going to reach for the stars, Ma," he told his mother one day. "And I'll bring one back for you."

Chapter 9

The Report

Dr. Bob did not earn much money as a part-time assistant professor. To make matters worse, he was always dipping into his own funds to buy supplies for his rocket experiments. Dr. Bob finally realized that he would have to have some financial backing if he were to continue with his research.

So he sat down and wrote out a report of what he had done in rocket research and what he hoped to do. He entitled the report "A Method of Reaching Extreme Altitudes." Then he began sending out the report to scientific organizations. He hoped that one of them might offer to put up some money.

The report came back time and again with polite turndowns. Dr. Bob was growing discouraged when one morning a letter arrived from the highly respected Smithsonian Institution in Washington, D.C.

His father was with him when he opened the letter. Nahum Goddard was alarmed as he saw his son's hands begin to shake.

"What's wrong?" Mr. Goddard asked. "Bad news?"

"No!" Dr. Bob said. "It's the most wonderful news in the world. The Smithsonian is interested in my work. They want to know how much money I need."

Dr. Bob was not certain what amount to ask for. But after much letter writing back and forth, the Smithsonian finally gave him a grant of five thousand dollars. He was delighted. Now he felt he was really on his way, but Dr. Bob was in for a disappointment. He had barely made a start in research with the funds from the Smithsonian when he was stopped short. World War I, which had been raging in Europe since 1914, now involved the United States.

Dr. Bob at once offered his services to Uncle Sam. His scientific talents were put to use by the U.S. Army Signal Corps. During 1917 and 1918, he helped develop a number of military weapons. One of the most promising was a rocket launcher. It was a tube through which a rocket could be fired, and it was lightweight enough to be carried and operated by one soldier. In later years this weapon was to be developed into the famous anti-tank bazooka of World War II.

Before Dr. Bob's rocket launcher could be put into production, the war ended. Dr. Bob was released by the Army, and he gladly went home to his mother and father in Worcester. He wasted little time in returning

to Clark University. There he began to pick up where
he had left off before the war.

Dr. Bob realized that a great deal had happened in
rocket research and in his own thinking since he had

first written his report for the Smithsonian in 1916. So, in order to bring the report up to date, he decided to rewrite it.

This he did, stressing especially his idea of a step rocket. He put into the rewritten report a description of what he believed such a rocket could do in the future. It would, he wrote, have the power to soar up through the atmosphere and enter outer space. The step rocket would be able to overcome the earth's gravity and keep on going through space until it actually landed on the moon.

Dr. Bob also suggested in his report that flash powder, of the kind used by photographers, be placed in the nose of such a rocket. He went so far as to suggest that if such a rocket were to hit the moon, the flash powder would go off and the burst of flame could be seen from telescopes on Earth.

The Smithsonian found the rewritten report very interesting. They published the paper late in 1919. It was just one of many scientific papers that went to science students and to libraries. It was not intended to be read by the public. But a newspaper reporter happened to see Dr. Bob's account. The reporter was struck by the moon rocket idea.

It stirred his imagination, and he saw how it could be made into a sensational news story. He immediately got to work and turned out a highly colored news account, twisting the truth all out of shape.

Newspaper after newspaper picked up the story of the scientist who was going to fly off to the moon in a rocket. Wild statements were followed by even wilder ones. In no time at all, Dr. Bob found himself on the front pages of newspapers across the land. He was called everything from a mad scientist to a crackpot and a faker. Cartoons were printed poking fun at him. Moon rocket jokes became the fashion. No one took Dr. Bob seriously.

He tried to explain that he had never meant that a manned rocket, or any rocket, could be sent to the moon right away. He had merely been pointing out what a future rocket might do. He also tried to answer fellow scientists who questioned the action-reaction principle of rocket flight. But no one seemed to listen.

The year 1920 was a terrible one for Dr. Bob. Not only was he jeered at, but he also suffered a deep personal loss. His mother finally lost her long fight against tuberculosis and died. He had known that she could not last much longer, but that did not lessen the heartbreak.

Upset and shaken, Dr. Bob tried to lose himself in his work at Clark University. Gradually the stir over the moon rocket faded out, and he was left alone and forgotten by the newspapers and by the public.

Chapter 10

Historymaker

At Clark University there was a pretty blond girl who was secretary to the president. Her name was Esther Kisk. She was saving her money to go to college, and when Dr. Bob needed someone to do typing for him, she agreed to take on the extra work.

Esther Kisk was bright and quick, and Dr. Bob was pleased to find that she had no trouble understanding his scientific language. He was also pleased when he discovered that she liked to talk about music and painting just as much as he did. Before long, the lanky professor and the young secretary were going to concerts and art exhibits together.

The fact that Esther Kisk was many years younger than Dr. Bob did not matter to either of them. They became close friends, and finally, on June 21, 1924, they were married.

Esther Goddard entered into the life of her professor-husband as if she had been reared for it. She not only cooked his meals and looked after the house, but she continued to do his typing and bookkeeping, helped out in the laboratory when necessary, and took on the thankless job of stretching Dr. Bob's slim salary to cover all expenses. In addition, she became the watchdog of her husband's health, doing her best to keep him from overworking.

This was one of her hardest tasks. Dr. Bob sensed that he was close to a breakthrough in his rocket experiments, and long hours of work meant nothing to him.

Up until this time, Dr. Bob had been using solid fuel for his rockets. But he had never been satisfied with the results. Now he decided to try a different type of fuel—a mixture of liquid oxygen (sometimes called lox) and gasoline. Great care had to be taken, as this fuel was highly explosive.

For five years, from 1920 until 1925, Dr. Bob designed and built a number of rockets with liquid-fuel motors. He tested each one thoroughly in the laboratory at Clark University. Then, early in 1926, he decided that he was ready for outdoor testing.

The first problem was to find a place outside of town and away from people so that no one would be hurt. Dr. Bob did not have to look far. Three miles to the south of Worcester, at Auburn, Massachusetts, was a farm owned by Miss Effie Ward. She was an old friend of the Goddard family. When Dr. Bob asked "Aunt" Effie if he could use part of her pasture for flight testing, she agreed.

Dr. Bob and his wife chose a site in a valley that was a safe distance away from the farmhouse and the barns. Here, several flight tests were attempted during the winter. Something always went wrong, and the rocket never left its launching frame. But it was different on the afternoon of March 16, 1926.

Early that day Dr. Bob and his assistant, Henry Sachs, loaded the latest rocket onto a trailer attached to their car. Then they drove out to the Ward farm for a test. It was cold and raw, and a thin blanket of snow still covered the ground.

A high windbreak made of sheet iron had already been set up at the launch site. Dr. Bob and his helper were grateful for its shelter as they put together the framework of the launching stand. When this was completed, the two men carefully placed the rocket into position, its nose pointed straight up.

The rocket was odd-looking by modern standards. It was ten feet long and had no outer cover. It looked like the skeleton of an up-to-date rocket. In front was a metal cylinder, and inside this cylinder was the rocket motor. Leading back from the motor were two thin pipes, five feet in length. The pipes were connected

at the rear to two small fuel tanks. One tank held
gasoline, and the other carried lox.

At one o'clock in the afternoon, Esther Goddard
drove out to the farm with Dr. Roope of the physics
department of Clark University. She brought along the

precious small motion-picture camera that she had managed to buy with nickels and dimes saved from her household money. Dr. Bob had appointed her official photographer.

By 2:30 in the afternoon, all was ready. Henry Sachs had a blowtorch attached to the end of a long pole. At Dr. Bob's signal, the torch was lighted. The valves of the fuel tanks were then turned on, and the blowtorch was lifted high into the air so that its flame went through an opening in the rocket's nose.

In a moment, the gasoline and lox caught fire with a loud *whoosh*. Flames gushed out of the exhaust nozzle. For an agonizing instant, the rocket remained motionless, as if anchored to the stand.

Suddenly it began to move upward. It moved slowly at first, then faster and faster, until it shot clear of the launching stand. It streaked like a bullet up into the sky.

Dr. Bob had his stopwatch in his hand. He and his wife and the other two men watched breathlessly.

The upward rush of the rocket did not last long. The roaring and the jet stream of fire stopped abruptly. The rocket curved over to the left and, still going at top speed, struck the snow-covered ground with a crash.

The flight had lasted less than three seconds. The distance covered had been no more than a hundred and eighty-four feet. The speed had been not much more than sixty miles an hour.

Yet on that chilly day in the spring of 1926, history had been made. The world's first liquid-fuel rocket had been successfully tested.

In the story of man's exploration of space, the day of March 16, 1926, was to become as important as December 17, 1903, when the Wright brothers made the first heavier-than-air flight.

A stone marker was placed at the launching site on the old Ward farm in Auburn, Massachusetts. It reads: SITE OF LAUNCHING OF WORLD'S FIRST LIQUID-PROPELLANT ROCKET BY DR. ROBERT H. GODDARD, MARCH 16, 1926.

Chapter 11

Flight West

Dr. Bob was pleased with the success of the test, of course. Yet he was not overly excited. As Esther Goddard was to say many years later on recalling the historic afternoon: "At the time of the flight, none of the four of us there had any sense of destiny. We had no feeling that this was something remarkable. We had hoped for a straight flight, and we didn't get it."

Less than a month later, on April 3, 1926, a second flight was made. This too was brief, lasting only four seconds, and was far from perfect. Yet it did prove that the first flight had not been a fluke.

Dr. Bob now decided to move the motor from the front of the rocket to the rear and to build much larger rockets. But the new size brought new troubles. The big rockets would not rise from their test stands.

After struggling to iron out the difficulties, Dr. Bob

finally went back to making smaller rockets again. On the day after Christmas in 1928, he was rewarded with a third successful flight. On July 17, 1929, the fourth liquid-propellant rocket was launched from the pasture land of Aunt Effie Ward's farm (and you will remember the commotion this one caused, from Chapter 1).

This famous rocket was the first to carry a payload. Packed into the nose of the sleek eleven-foot rocket was a barometer to record atmospheric pressures, a thermometer to register temperatures, and a small camera. The camera was to photograph the readings on both instruments when the rocket reached the top of its climb.

The launching that sultry afternoon was the best yet. The rocket soared up from the stand with a bellowing roar that echoed like thunder across the hot, still air of the countryside. At a height of almost two hundred feet, the rocket leveled off from its straight-up climb. It streaked noisily along, parallel to the ground, for over two hundred feet, spitting out a trail of scarlet flame. Then, when its fuel was used up, the rocket dived to the ground.

Dr. Bob was delighted with the test. So was his wife, who had photographed every moment of it with her movie camera. So were the four men who had helped Dr. Bob get the rocket ready.

But their satisfaction was wiped away by the sudden

arrival at the test site of policemen and newspaper reporters, who had come in response to the false alarm that an airplane had crashed.

The last thing Dr. Bob wanted was to have the newspapers printing wild stories about him and his moon rocket. But like it or not, he was back in the headlines with a splash. What made it even worse was the official ruling that banned him from making any more rocket tests in his home state of Massachusetts.

Yet the luck that seemed to Dr. Bob to be so bad in the end turned out to be good. For among the millions of people who read the news accounts of the "crazy scientist and his moon rocket blowing up" was a certain young man named Charles Lindbergh.

Colonel Charles Lindbergh was very famous. Just two years before, in 1927, he had won world acclaim when he had flown alone across the Atlantic Ocean from New York to Paris.

On reading about Dr. Goddard and his rocket, Colonel Lindbergh began to wonder what really lay behind the newspaper accounts. He decided to travel to Worcester and find out.

Colonel Lindbergh called on Dr. Bob, and the two men had a long talk. Dr. Bob told the famous pilot all about what he had done and his plans for the future. He showed him, too, the movies of the rocket tests that his wife had taken.

Colonel Lindbergh was impressed. When he left, he

was convinced that Dr. Bob's work was so important that it should go on. The colonel went to the wealthy Guggenheim family and told them about the New England professor who was years ahead of his time. The Guggenheims had given great amounts of money to aid many aviation projects.

After an investigation, they offered Dr. Bob a large grant of money to continue and expand his work. The grant could not have come at a better time, for the funds from the Smithsonian Institution were almost used up.

Now that Dr. Bob could no longer do his experiments in Massachusetts, he set out to find the perfect place for rocket research. He found it in the wide-open state of faraway New Mexico.

So it was that, in the summer of 1930, Dr. Bob, his wife, and four assistants went to New Mexico and settled near the town of Roswell.

Dr. Bob wrote in his diary: "In July 1930, we went to Roswell, N.M., and had the shop running by October, and had a flight of about half a mile as a thrilling climax to the year in December 1930."

The flight was indeed thrilling. The rocket streaked to the astonishing height of two thousand feet, and its speed was not sixty miles an hour, or ninety, or even one hundred. On this fifth official test, the top speed was registered at *five hundred miles an hour*!

Chapter 12

The Space Age

There were reverses and disappointments ahead for Dr. Bob, of course, and many failures too. But now he was over the hump. His rockets began to soar higher and faster, and so did his hopes.

On March 28, 1935, an altitude of 4,800 feet was reached. On May 31 of the same year, this record height was boosted to 7,500 feet. But what was truly amazing was the fact that this rocket traveled at the incredible speed of seven hundred miles an hour, which is very close to the speed of sound.

More and more people began to hear of the soft-spoken professor with the slow smile and the fast-traveling rockets. Airmen, both military and civilian, came to Roswell to see what was going on. Many arrived clearly expecting to find a fake but went away deeply impressed.

Letters arrived from foreign scientists, notably

Germans, asking questions about the *Herr Doktor*'s rockets. Dr. Bob answered all of the queries. He had nothing to hide. After all, every bit of information about his basic rocket patents could be had by simply writing to Washington and enclosing ten cents.

Yet for all of the gathering interest, Dr. Bob found it impossible to get the U.S. War Department to take rocketry seriously. After World War II had broken out in Europe, he went to Washington to give his views on the use of rockets as weapons. But the military high command still would not consider such newfangled ideas.

It soon became evident that Germany, under the control of Hitler and the Nazis, had thought otherwise. That country had been hard at work on rocket research for some time and had developed a deadly type of rocket weapon called the V-2.

The V-2 was forty-six feet long and could reach a height of seventy miles. It carried two thousand pounds of high explosives in its nose. The power of this weapon was shown when the Nazis launched a savage rocket attack on the city of London, England, in 1944. The rockets were shot from hidden ramps in France. Within minutes, they were screaming down on the capital of Great Britain at over three thousand miles an hour.

Diagrams of the German bomb were sent to the United States from England. Dr. Bob was called in to inspect them. In almost every detail, he found that the

German rocket was very similar to the basic rocket he had patented so long ago. It seemed quite clear, and was later admitted by German scientists, that they had done considerable "borrowing" from Dr. Goddard.

When the United States entered the war, Dr. Bob closed his laboratory and left his testing grounds. He began work for the U.S. Navy on a type of rocket motor. But his health was now failing.

After a physical examination, he learned that he would have to have a serious throat operation. In the summer of 1945, he entered a hospital in Baltimore, Maryland. The operation was successful, and after a while Dr. Goddard, though weak, was able to sit up and scribble out some notes about future work.

But suddenly he took a turn for the worse. His wife, Esther, was hurriedly sent for. On August 10, 1945, at the age of sixty-three, Dr. Bob died.

There is a saying that a prophet is not honored in his own country. It might be said of scientists too, especially of Dr. Goddard.

Yet after his death, the United States did its best to make up for its long neglect. Honors were heaped on the memory of the New England physics professor. In his name, Dr. Goddard's widow was presented with the country's highest decoration for civilians, the Congressional Gold Medal, and with aviation's greatest award, the Langley Gold Medal.

Great research laboratories, like the Goddard Space Center at Greenbelt, Maryland, and the Goddard

Institute of Space Study in New York City, were named for him. The government saw to it that overdue payments for the use of the Goddard rocket patents were made to his estate.

Then on July 2, 1962, the House of Representatives passed a bill to establish a day of national honor for Dr. Robert H. Goddard. The date is March 16, the very day when, in 1926, Dr. Goddard launched the world's first liquid-fuel rocket.

In the years that have followed, bigger and more powerful rockets have roared into the sky in steady procession. Satellites have been sent spinning through space to relay back messages of weather conditions, of magnetic fields, and of the dangers of radiation. Rocket-propelled spaceships have taken men around the earth. Space probes have been sent beyond the reaches of our solar system. Astronauts have landed on the moon. Mars, perhaps, will be next.

There is no limit to what the rockets that Dr. Bob started can do, no limit to where they will take us. As young Bob Goddard said in his high school graduation oration so long ago: "The dream of yesterday is the hope of today and the reality of tomorrow."

How Rockets Have Grown

On March 16, 1926, the space age began. This was the day that Robert Goddard launched his first liquid-fuel rocket. Rockets have been getting bigger ever since. You can see below how much they have grown. The first drawing shows a man standing beside Goddard's 1926 rocket. The last drawing shows the Saturn-V, which launched men to the moon. In between are rockets that have lifted missiles, satellites, space probes, and manned vehicles.

Why do we need to make bigger and bigger rockets? To lift larger and larger loads. A 1929 Goddard rocket

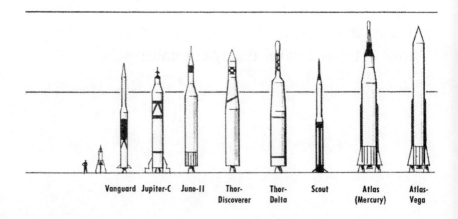

Vanguard Jupiter-C Juno-II Thor-Discoverer Thor-Delta Scout Atlas (Mercury) Atlas-Vega

carried the first payload—a thermometer, a barometer, and a small camera. The Saturn-V lifted 90,000 pounds of men and equipment. You can see that the weight of what we send into space depends on the power of the rocket that boosts it up there.

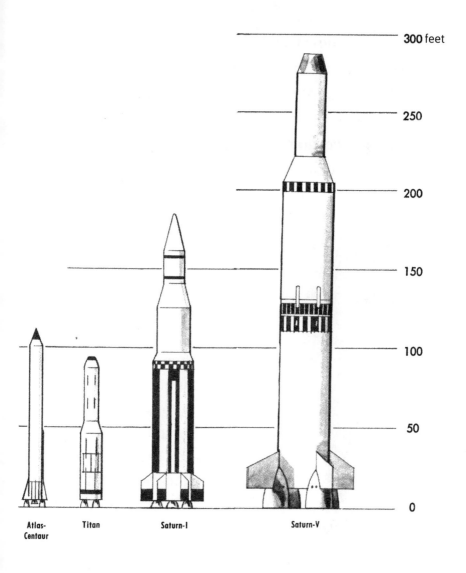

300 feet

250

200

150

100

50

0

Atlas-Centaur   Titan   Saturn-I   Saturn-V

Higher and Higher

Now you know why Robert Goddard is called the father of the space age. His rockets began man's climb into the vast space beyond our earth. Since Goddard's death, we have put rockets to many uses. What new jobs are rockets doing? Let's begin close to the ground and go upward, looking at the work of higher and higher flying rockets.

Rocket Belt

What holds this man up? He wears a rocket belt. Look at the nozzle that points down over his shoulder. There is one just like it on his other shoulder. Out of these two nozzles shoot two invisible jets of steam—powerful enough to lift him and his equipment.

Twin tanks on the man's back carry fuel for the rockets that produce these jet streams. In his hands he holds the controls.

Rocket Ships

Tucked under the wing of a giant jet plane is the world's first

spacecraft. Its name: X-15. Is it a plane? Yes. Its job is to find out what space is like for men and vehicles.

After the X-15 is launched, its pilot starts the rocket engine, and it streaks upward. In two minutes its fuel is spent, and the craft coasts upward to the edge of

space at 4,000 miles an hour. Then it glides to Earth, and the pilot lands it.

Earth Satellites

Communications: Early Bird receives and sends telephone calls and TV programs between the U.S. and Europe.

Navigation: Transit satellites guide ships, planes, and submarines located anywhere around the world.

Military: Midas satellites can detect missile launchings. Other military satellites take around-the-clock photographs of the entire world.

Weather: Tiros IX rolls like a drum around the earth, taking pictures of the clouds below it. These pictures help in forecasting weather.

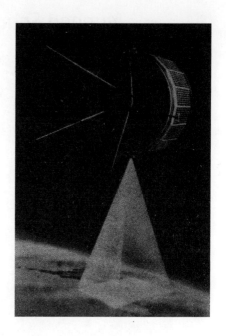

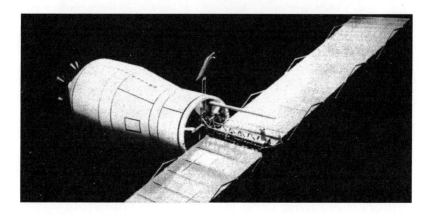

Fact-finding: Pegasus spreads its wings to count dust particles in space. Facts like these tell us more about space.

Manned Space Vehicles

Inside a space capsule model, engineers are making safety tests. The capsule must protect astronauts from great noise and heat during firing. It must help protect them from great pressure as the boosting rocket speeds upward against the force of gravity. Once they are above gravity in airless space, they must be protected from lack of pressure, lack of oxygen to breathe, lack of heat on the shady side, too much heat on the sunny side, radiation, and meteorites.

These boys are taking an imaginary flight in a model of a Mercury space capsule. They feel like astronauts, for they are watching a film of the earth 100 miles below. In years to come, they may make real space flights in real spaceships.

And so may you!

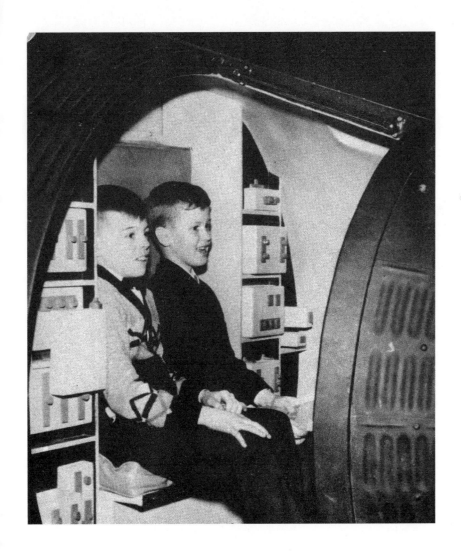